D1216596

Happy Birthday. Marc!   July 16, 2010

♡ Laurel

The Amazing Faith of Texas
Common Ground on Higher Ground

1 Corinthians

Love is patient, love is kind. It does not envy, it does not boast, it is not proud. It is not rude, it is not self-seeking, it is not easily angered, it keeps no record of wrongs. Love does not delight in evil but rejoices with the truth. It always protects, always trusts, always hopes, always perseveres!

... And now these three remain: faith, hope and love. But the greatest of these is love!

♡ Laurel

THE AMAZING FAITH OF TEXAS

Common Ground on Higher Ground

By ROY SPENCE with the People of Texas

Stories collected and edited by MIKE BLAIR

Photography by RANDAL FORD

Copyright © 2006 by GSD&M LP
All rights reserved
Printed in Singapore

First University of Texas Press edition, 2009

Requests for permission to reproduce material from this work should be sent to:
    Permissions
    University of Texas Press
    P.O. Box 7819
    Austin, TX 78713-7819
    www.utexas.edu/utpress/about/bpermission.html

∞ The paper used in this book meets the minimum requirements
of ANSI/NISO Z39.48-1992 (R1997) (Permanence of Paper).

Library of Congress Cataloging-in-Publication Data

Roy Spence, 1948–

The Amazing Faith of Texas:
Common Ground on Higher Ground
By Roy Spence with the People of Texas

Stories collected and edited by Mike Blair
Photography by Randal Ford, © 2006
Book design by Craig Denham

    p. cm.
    ISBN 978-0-292-72176-0
    I. Religion 2. General interest.

Library of Congress Control Number: 2006924026

Texas has always had a tremendous array of cultures. As native Texans, my colleagues and I have been immersed in this unique diversity ever since we can remember. It was this deep understanding that led us to create the now-legendary "Don't Mess with Texas" campaign in the 1980s and the Texas Tourism campaign, "Texas. It's Like a Whole Other Country." It is clear to me that while we all come from different regions and cultures, we are bound together because we are Texans — native or not — and we always come together when we see a common purpose.

Yet in the past years, it seemed that when it came to religion and faith, more was being reported about what divides Texans than what unites us. As a person who has spent most of my life trying in some small way to bring people together for the common good, that worried me. So we gathered a small group of Texans together and decided to get in a Winnebago and crisscross Texas, loaded with cameras and sound equipment, to uncover the truth. We sought to find out if what unites us as a family of faith is deeper than what divides us. The results of that journey you now hold in your hands.

I am not a pastor, but I am a person who loves God and God's people, so I was heartened to find out that no matter what you hear secondhand, the people of Texas are united. Not on everything. But when it comes to faith, Texans are very devoted to their own and yet share an amazing amount of common ground on higher ground with others. So enjoy. And celebrate *The Amazing Faith of Texas.*

The Amazing Faith of Texas

I.

COMMON GROUND FOUND IN FAITH

TEXANS ARE UNITED IN THE DEEP AND ABIDING FAITH that there is a supreme being. And while different Texans believe and worship in different ways, there is no doubt that Texans are united as a family of faith. That unity is also brought to life in the amazing tolerance and respect of how their fellow Texans practice their individual faiths. Faith. Tolerance. Respect.

2.

COMMON GROUND FOUND IN THE GOLDEN RULE

TEXANS ASPIRE TO PRACTICE the Golden Rule. In every region and religion of Texas, people have some version of the Golden Rule to guide them as their North Star. And once again Texans are united — united in their self-admission of not always living up to the principle of the Golden Rule. But make no mistake about it: The Golden Rule is alive and well in Texas.

3.

COMMON GROUND FOUND IN VALUES

TEXANS SEEK TO LIVE A LIFE of compassion, charity, humility and forgiveness. We listened closely and heard the calling of all the faiths in Texas guiding us to live by several common-ground values. There are four that unite most Texans. It is simply amazing that these four paths celebrated in each religion are so universal: compassion, charity, humility and forgiveness.

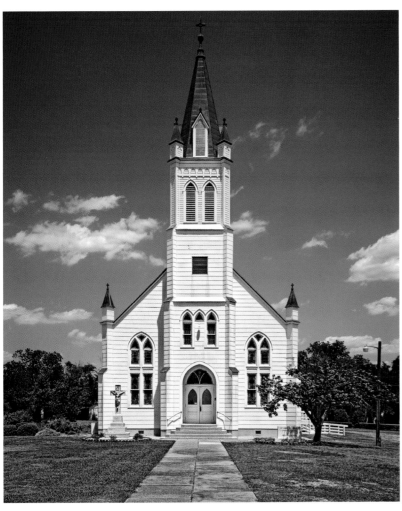

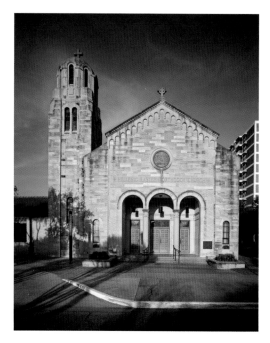  

"God is too big to fit inside one religion."

UNKNOWN

I.

COMMON GROUND

FOUND IN FAITH

"You can't preach the Word and not live it. Too much of religion is takin' and not enough about givin'."

Ron Conatser says, "There's two things I don't like...religion and red tape." That might sound a bit odd from a man who preaches the gospel every Sunday at the Risin Sun Cowboy Church outside of Trinity, Texas. The Risin Sun sits on a two-lane blacktop back in the pine trees of East Texas. If you didn't see the sign, you'd think it was a dance hall. Fifteen years ago, that's what it was. Ron Conatser was a rodeo rider then.

"I'm 69 years old, and I've spent my whole life as a cowboy and over 40 years in the rodeo. Back in '78, I was workin' a rodeo in San Antonio, and I made a decision at a little old cowboy church one mornin' durin' the rodeo. It was in one of those little clown rooms back behind the buckin' chutes, the only place they'd let us have church. I made a decision that day to do what God wanted me to do, whatever it was. Next week I was in Houston judging a rodeo, and between performances I went over to the Astrohall to cowboy church, and there were three or four hundred people there, but the preacher hadn't shown up. I just opened my Bible and stood up and started preachin'. Evidently, God wanted me to spread the Word. Been preachin' ever since. Bought me this dance hall in '91 and got busy preachin' the Word of God to whoever walks through the door. We're a Word church. No denomination. Just a place where people can come just the way they are and worship God. Pretty simple." No religion. No red tape.

"You can't preach the Word and not live it. Too much of religion is takin' and not enough about givin'. You take the Dead Sea. It's dead because there's something goin' into it but nothin' comin' out. We're supposed to give, and if we don't ever give, we just get dead. That's my faith talkin', and faith is more important than anything, I reckon."

RON CONATSER *Rodeo Cowboy. Preacher. Texan.*

"FAITH IS LIKE RIDING IN A CAR WITH RAY CHARLES DRIVING. IF YOU CAN'T RIDE IN A CAR WITH RAY CHARLES DRIVING, MAN, YOU AIN'T GOT FAITH."

"I RAN A MOTEL FOR 15 YEARS. You know, one of those places that rents rooms by the hour. But my heart started changing in the late '80s, and in 1990 I had me one of those sort of radical conversion experiences and became a Christian. I didn't quite understand it, but I knew my heart was different somehow."

Pastor Rudy Rasmus talks slowly and thoughtfully when you ask him about his faith. Like someone who has thought long and deeply about it.

"I began to feel a need to do something to help people, which was an overwhelming experience because prior to that, I only felt the need to earn a profit from people. I discovered that I was experiencing a call to ministry, so I enrolled in seminary classes and began to learn a little more about faith. A year later, I was looking for a church, and my pastor at the time [Kirbyjon Caldwell] told me to check out this old abandoned church here in downtown Houston to see what kind of potential it had. I pulled up and saw all these homeless folks just everywhere. I called my wife and said, 'Baby, this is the place.' So now we have this church [St. John's Methodist], and we serve the homeless and people with HIV. We don't try to fix 'em. We just love 'em. It's a heartwarming gig.

"As we move into this part of this century, we're seeing that there are a whole lot more similarities in our faith experiences than there are differences. I've never been spooked by that, though. I've always been cool with Muslims and Buddhists. We all have something to learn from each other. We really do. It's like I tell my friends, 'If you don't think enough about your path to want to convince me to get on it, I wouldn't think much of your path.' I think a lot of my path. And I think a lot of yours."

PASTOR RUDY RASMUS *Methodist. Preacher. Texan.*

"We must learn to embrace our differences and learn from them."

"For me every day is an opportunity to learn so much that I don't know about other cultures, other faith traditions and about myself. I have an obligation to help build bridges, to help understand each other, to respect our differences as human beings and to embrace and learn from these differences."

Nelin Hudani escaped the killings in Idi Amin's Uganda when she was nine. Nelin is a Shia Imami Ismaili Sufi Muslim. If there is hesitation in anyone about the Muslim faith at this time, it is put to rest if you meet Nelin. She could tell you that there are radical fringes in all faiths. But it is not in her nature to cast doubts, to talk in negatives. Nelin is a child of peace, a child of God, and it radiates from her like a rainbow.

"I will tell you a story about how God works in my life. I was diagnosed with terminal cancer in 1992 and was told that I had less than a month to live. After my second relapse in December 1993, I received a phone call from my father telling me that my dear grandmother had suffered a massive stroke. She was the love of my life. Though I had Stage IV lymphoma, I rose from my bed and flew to Vancouver to be by her side. On the plane there, I prayed continuously to God to please not take her from me. The moment I arrived at her bedside, I forgot completely how ill I was. I decided I would stay by her side and share her pain. What I didn't realize as I spent those hours, days and months with her in the hospital as she healed was that I was healing as well. My cancer completely disappeared, and I know now that my grandmother took this stroke upon herself to get me out of bed to come share the journey with her in order for me to heal. I learned so much during that time. About myself, about God, about love, about faith. My grandmother lived for five more years. I am more alive than ever."

NELIN HUDANI *Survivor. Muslim. Texan.*

"For those who believe, no explanation is needed.
For those who do not believe, no explanation is possible."

ST. IGNATIUS LOYOLA

"GOD IS AN EQUAL-OPPORTUNITY LISTENER."

"CATHOLICS AND JEWS ARE ALMOST THE SAME, but the Catholic mother says, 'If you don't eat that, I'll kill you,' and the Jewish mother says, 'If you don't eat that, I'll kill myself.'"

Daniel Russ is a comedian. He is also a Jew. But he will tell you that nobody has a monopoly on truth. He believes that there are many ways to have a relationship with God, and no one religion has a lock on that.

"I have a wonderful relationship with God, and I think ultimately your relationship with God has got to be personal. I think that whenever you abdicate your spiritual growth to an organization, God's a little disappointed. Here's one way I put my head around it: In the West, God is transcendent of the world, and in the East, God is imminent to the world. One God is sort of a person in the sky, and the other is that God that is imbued in everything we do. I think that both are probably true because God is, by definition, infinite and hard to understand. I don't believe in God for mental or rational reasons. I believe in God for emotional reasons because I've seen God work in my own life. So I pray all the time. I just don't ask permission from a man on a pulpit to talk to God. God is an equal-opportunity listener. He listens directly to everybody.

"We're all like missiles that are looking for a target. We're always trying to figure out — what is it all about? And I think that everybody has the ability inside them to find the answers that are right for them."

DANIEL RUSS *Comedian. Jew. Texan.*

"GOD IS THE BOSS AND

I'M JUST AN EMPLOYEE."

"I WORKED IN A MONASTERY WHEN I WAS YOUNG, and I remember when I was 15 being attracted to the monastic life. I wasn't sure though. I felt this great attraction for it, but at the same time, I was in darkness. I didn't know where God was. I prayed that He would show me His will, what He wanted me to do with my life. I remember walking the streets in the rain, crying. I was like, 'Where are You, God? Just show me.' Later on after I joined the monastery, I laughed as I realized why I couldn't see God. He was behind me pushing me every step of the way."

Sister Angela is a nun in the Order of the Poor Clares, founded in 1212 by St. Clare and St. Francis of Assisi. If you visit her monastery just north of Brenham, do so in the springtime. The Monastery of St. Clare raises miniature horses, and springtime brings the foals. If you want to see the joy in God's creation, it is exemplified in a 20-pound horse.

"I can pray anywhere. I can go out in the woods, in the fields with the horses. But it's a different sense when you walk into a church; you're just kind of awed, and a hush comes over you and a kind of sense of silence and mystery and awe. In my religion, we have Jesus who came and lived among us and walked among us as our brother. Then on the other hand, you have the Trinity, the King of Kings and Lord of Lords who created the world and the universe and will reign forever. It's like, 'Wow, this is an awesome, untouchable God.' I think you have to approach God both ways. At least I do.

"God is the boss and I'm just an employee. He puts hurdles in my way every day, and I've got to respond as best I can — but when it's all said and done, He's the one in control, and I don't have to lie awake worrying about things. I just do my job and turn the rest over to Him. Makes life so much easier."

SISTER ANGELA *Catholic Nun. Horse Breeder. Texan.*

"Come, let us walk in the light of the Lord."

Isaiah 2:5, ESV

"No matter how much you might question God, He is there."

"I like to think of my songs as conversations between me and God. And it's a beautiful experience. Because no matter what you're struggling with in your life, music is the universal language."

Casey McPherson is a musician. He will tell you that his music is a source of peace for him, a place where he can go to make sense of the things that happen to us.

"My father committed suicide six years ago. My brother followed him a year later. I mean, I was living in a white-picket-fence existence up to that point. All of a sudden, it was all blown out of the water. I think when something like this happens, it tends to move you both away from and toward God, if that makes any sense. The anger makes you question Him and be angry with Him, but that only serves to move you toward Him. I made a record right after my father's death, and listening back to it, I hear a lot of asking: 'Why did this happen? Why does God let bad things happen to good people?' I had to face a lot of truth as far as what I really believed. So I began to look closer at my relationship with God, and I realized I was just not where He wanted me to be. I decided to use this tragedy and whatever healing I've gotten over these last six years and bring it to my music to try to help anyone who's experiencing pain and not really knowing how to deal with it.

"What I took from this experience is that no matter how much you might question God when bad things happen, no matter how angry you might get, you can still have faith that He is there. There is still that voice. And that is reassuring."

CASEY McPHERSON   *Musician. Christian. Texan.*

"God was in every foxhole."

"I remember sitting in a foxhole in the Ardennes forest. It was freezing. The artillery was crashing all around us; bullets were flying; a Catholic priest came by to bless us; and the guy in the foxhole with me said, 'Where's your gun?' The priest held up his cross and said, 'Right here.'"

Eduardo Salmon was a young man when he took his faith in God into the hell of World War II. He was a lot older when he came back home to West Texas.

"We were fighting for our freedom. I believe every human being has a right to be free. And that includes the freedom to worship however we choose. I am a Catholic; I find great strength in my faith. You may be a Jew or a Muslim or a Hindu, and you have the right to worship God in your way. I don't understand why it bothers some people that someone may worship differently than them. Why is it wrong? I know that when we were fighting in that war, there were people of all faiths in those foxholes. God was right there with each one of us. And with His blessings, many of us came home.

"God doesn't care how we worship Him. Only that we do. Why should we make an issue of it?"

EDUARDO SALMON *WWII Vet. Catholic. Texan.*

"Faith is a mystery expressed in action."

"There's a great deal of beauty in the mystery of faith. I've talked with a lot of people over the years who have tried to reason their way to God. And my suggestion is that you don't want a God that you can fully understand. We desire and we need a God who is beyond our understanding. You can have a relationship with Him, but you can't fully understand Him. To define that mystery or to try to box it in betrays it and ultimately impinges on the beauty of it. We ought to be comfortable with and enjoy the mystery of it. Just roll around in it a bit."

Mac Richard is the pastor at Lake Hills Church in Austin. He is a young man who speaks with the wisdom of age. His faith is strong. His energy is magnetic.

"The common ground for all religions is actually the common ground for all of humanity, and that is a need for God. It's not accidental that God says in the book of Ecclesiastes, I placed eternity in the heart of man. We have a need and a longing for something beyond ourselves, something beyond the immediate. I believe with everything in me that the only answer for that need is a relationship with God. And when you walk in a relationship with God, you pursue Him with all your heart and your soul and your mind, and you love Him with everything you've got."

MAC RICHARD *Pastor. Christian. Texan.*

"I LIKE TO THINK I CARRY MY CHURCH AROUND WITH ME."

"WE ALL HAVE OUR PRAYERS ANSWERED IN ONE WAY OR ANOTHER, but we may not always recognize the answer because it may not come in the way we expect. But when I am in that place that allows me to be in touch, I am always certain of the answer."

Ginger Blair is one of those human beings who seem to manifest all that is good about spirituality. She will tell you that her faith doesn't necessarily fit in a box, that it is universal. But it is apparent that it comes from a place of deep commitment.

"From as early as I can remember, I've had a deep connection with whatever you wish to call it...God, universal spirit, higher energy. And I don't think you necessarily have to go to church to have this connection. I like to think that I carry my church around with me. In my heart. I call it living with God. And when you live with God, you come from a centered place. In this world where things are so scattered, your energy is constantly being pulled to the outside. It's in these moments, when you are preoccupied with what is around you, that you lose your connection to God and lose your ability to recognize the guidance He is sending.

"We spend so much time living in our heads instead of in our hearts. When we are in our heads, we are thinking about what we have to do next, what we should have done differently, where we have to be at seven. That breaks our connection with God. Think of it like a giant receptor, like a radio station. When you are in your head, the station has static and doesn't come in as clearly. When you are in your heart, you are right on the dial."

GINGER BLAIR   *Universal Faith. Tuned In. Texan.*

"Don't mix your thoughts with your heart. Because your heart is always right."

"My grandfather always said, 'Don't ever let anyone tell you that you have to go sit down and be taught to do this. You were born into it. You are not taught.'"

Louis Beareagle is a full-blooded Mescalero Apache shaman. He is exactly what you might expect a Native American shaman to be. Very wise. Very spiritual. Very in touch with nature, with the seen and the unseen.

"I was raised by my grandparents. My grandfather was a shaman, and I was raised in it, around it; I breathed it, ate it. Whenever we would go to visit a family to pray and do the things we do, my grandfather would sometimes turn it over to me — and I would take over the prayers and things, and it would be very natural to me. Very comfortable. I was in step with him without any coaching. It just came naturally. It came from my heart, and my grandfather would always say, 'Don't mix your thoughts with your heart because your heart is always right.' We should always listen to our elders, be a sponge, soak up what they have to offer, because they speak from the wisdom of time.

"To me, when I follow my heart, it is the Creator speaking. The Creator always has something in mind for you, and you don't challenge it. You just go, as they say, with the flow. People come to me and say, 'Why is my life upside down? Why is this happening to me?' I say to them, 'The Creator is putting these obstacles in front of you to challenge you. It is up to you to make it over these obstacles.'

"What you own here is not really yours because everything belongs to the Creator. We're just vessels on this Mother Earth, and we do what we have to do to get along — but we should respect the Creator and Mother Earth as we go. And our faith is what carries us. Faith is what I believe, not what you believe. Because your faith may be going about it in a different way than mine, but eventually, we all wind up facing the same direction."

LOUIS BEAREAGLE *Native American. Shaman. Wise Man.*

"Take the first step in faith. You don't have to see
the whole staircase, just take the first step."

Dr. Martin Luther King, Jr.

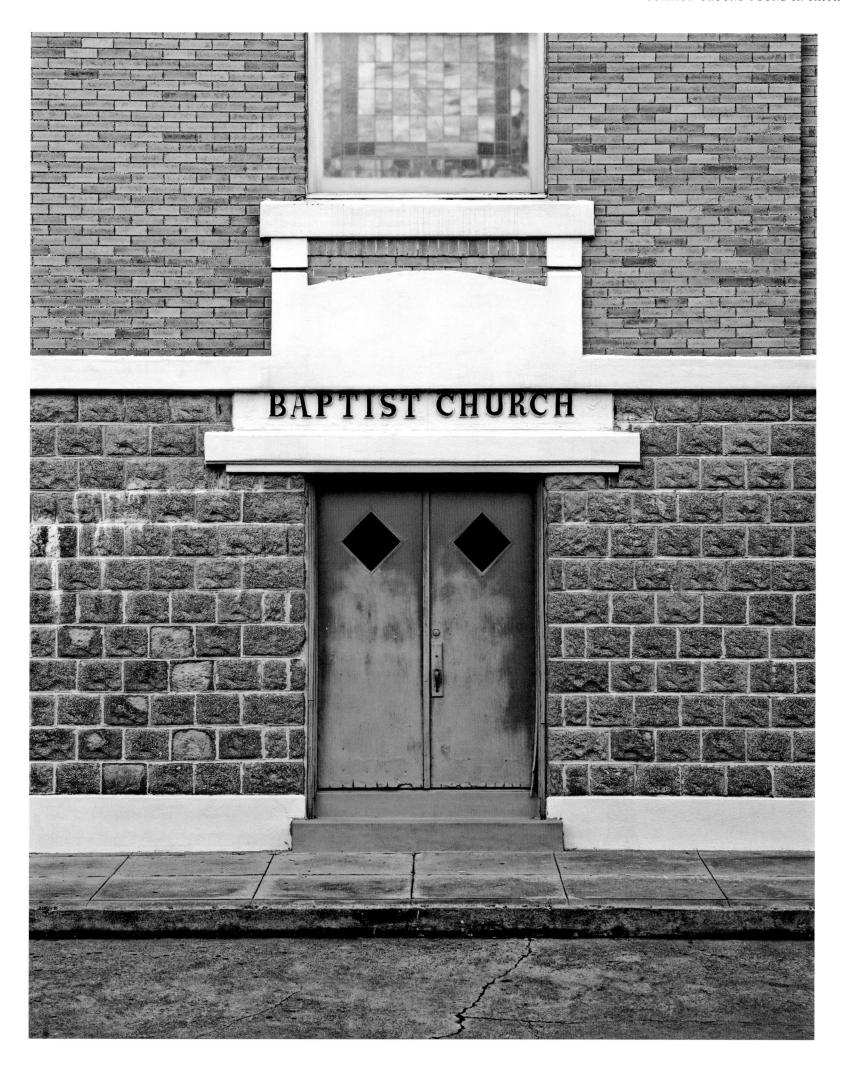

DELICIAE MEAE ESSE CUM FILIIS HOMINUM · PROV. 8. ·

"We Texans never give up.

Neither does God. Could it

be that God is a Texan?"

"My husband was born in a different faith than me. By the time we met, he was almost an atheist. And I remember praying to God, 'What have I gotten myself into?' The answer I got was to not let the word *God* get in the way. He believed the same thing I did, but he had a lot of prejudice against the word *God*."

Lynn Kindler is one of those people who simply radiate joy, one of those people you want to hug just because.

"I'm one of those people who test God a lot, and He is always up to the test. I fell asleep at the wheel one time after drinking a little too much. Well...a lot too much. I drove off an overpass and ended up partly on a train track at night. And a train was coming. I remember lying there and feeling the blood and the feeling of shock and seeing the train coming and saying, 'Oh, God, please help me,' and I heard a very reassuring voice say to me, 'Climb into the backseat and get out of the car and get up the hill because nobody is going to find you, and the shock will kill you if the train doesn't.' Something helped me up that hill and saved my life.

"If you think about it, God is always doing everything in God's power to help us have faith. Something happens to you, and God says, 'Did you see that, Lynn? You didn't see that? Here, let me show you something else.' I can look back on my life and see so many instances where God was there for me. And the more I think about it, the deeper my faith becomes."

LYNN KINDLER *Seeker. Believer. Texan.*

"FAITH HAS A FACE FOR ME NOW."

"I NEVER THOUGHT TOO MUCH ABOUT MY FAITH UNTIL MY ACCIDENT. Six years ago, I broke my neck and was paralyzed from the neck down. Before the accident, I considered myself a good Catholic. I did all the things a Catholic is supposed to do. So I had my religion. But I'm not sure I had my faith. I think I had the volume turned down, you know?"

Jared Dunten speaks with the understanding of someone who has had his faith severely tested. "What this experience has given me is a true appreciation for the temporariness of it all. And I definitely walk a lot closer to God now. Faith has a face for me now. I see it in everyone who has come together to help me, all these people from all different faiths who have been there for me — some were Catholic, but most were who-knows-what religion. They all came together to help me and my family through this. I sometimes think the accident happened for a reason. Don't get me wrong — I can't wait to not be paralyzed. But to be quite honest, the journey is where it's at. This might sound strange, but it has been a beautiful time. The people I've met, the things I've done, the things I've seen because of it. It really has been beautiful."

JARED DUNTEN *Catholic. Paralyzed — Temporarily. Texan.*

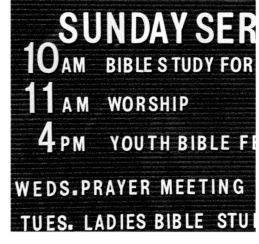

"Here's the thing about God. He doesn't care
how you get the message as long as you get it."

UNKNOWN

"Let's all get real quiet."

"To me faith is the realization that my intellect is only going to get me so far. At best it's an infinitesimal fraction of where God wants me to be. At worst it gets in the way of love."

Haley Rushing is one of those people who make you smile just to look at her. You can feel the love flow from her. You can hear the love in her words.

"When you think of some of the things that Jesus calls us to do — love your neighbor as yourself…judge not, lest you be judged…do unto others as you would have done to you — how do you actually do that? In my faith, Christian Contemplative, we are taught that our personalities get in the way of love. The ego is out for power, affection, esteem, survival…desires that conflict with what we are called to do. The spiritual journey is all about transcending the ego — if only for brief moments — so that we can truly experience love.

"I went on my first silent retreat in Belton, Texas, a few years ago. On day one, your mind is occupied with the jibber-jabber of daily life. You look at the other people, and your mind tells you stories about them — 'she's more spiritual than me'; 'she was rude to me last week'; 'that person will never be able to keep it quiet.' By day two, you start to get tired of hearing your own thoughts, and they begin to quiet down. After a few days, a miraculous thing happens. All the personalities and egos that showed up on day one have faded away, and all you can see when you look around are fellow spirits. All the judgment melts away. That's when you can start to truly love one another. We do so much scrambling and seeking and talking about God, but — for me — the only time I truly find God is when I calm down and shut up. Try it sometime. Just be silent. See if you don't start seeing and hearing God more clearly.

"The Hindus talk about everybody going up the same mountaintop. God is at the top of the mountain, and there are many paths that lead to the top, and depending on the culture that you grow up in, it's going to determine which path you decide to take. And to me the value of all the world religions is providing the paths that feel right to individuals all over the world."

HALEY RUSHING   *Christian Contemplative. Mother of Twins. Texan.*

"GOD IS BEYOND OUR CAPACITY TO DEFINE."

"SPIRITUALITY IS THE MORE GENERAL TERM FOR THE SEARCH for transcendent meaning in life. Religion is the most important expression of reality for those who affirm a belief in God and who feel called by a higher power to a vocation in life."

Rabbi Samuel Karff was called to that higher vocation. Rabbi Karff is Rabbi Emeritus at Congregation Beth Israel in Houston. When you hear him speak, you hear, no matter what your religion, the voice of a calm man. A fair man. A kind man. The voice of wisdom. The voice of reason. The voice of tolerance.

"It is the human spirit that quests for meaning, and it's the meaning of life that sustains that will to live. The will to live is not instinctive in human beings. It can be lost. Certainly for those of us who are religious, part of the will to live — a very important part of it — is linked to the one who gave us life and who gave us a mission in our life.

"God is beyond our capacity to define because to define is to limit. God cannot be controlled, and therefore God cannot be defined, yet our religious traditions guide us in our attempt to experience God's presence and discern God's will. We are invited to trust that beyond the mystery, there is meaning. Our faith is a recognition that there are realities that cannot be adequately expressed in scientific terms, but they are extraordinarily real and extraordinarily important. Faith is the belief in the reality of the unseen."

RABBI SAMUEL KARFF   *Wise Man. Kind Man. Texan.*

"Where there is hatred, let me sow love.
Where there is injury, pardon. Where there is doubt, faith."

ST. FRANCIS OF ASSISI

"MY RELIGION IS IN THE TREES."

"WE WEREN'T RAISED IN ANY PARTICULAR RELIGION although we'd go to an Episcopal church on Easter Sunday. And when I was four, I asked my parents, 'Why don't we go to church every Sunday?' They were like, 'Well, religion is a very important thing, and we think when you're old enough to be able to think about these things critically, you should be able to choose your own.' It was the same answer to the question 'Why didn't you get me baptized?' And my mom was like, 'Well, we weren't going to make that decision for you. That's a pretty big deal.'"

Anna Huff lives in Terlingua, Texas, with her husband, Dave. She's a mail-order minister and an artist, and if this were the '60s, you might call her a hippie.

"I can remember, when I did go to church as a child, wondering where God was. I'd look for Him in the rafters, in the stained glass. I was confused. Because I knew that this was a place of worship, but I couldn't see God there. But I remember feeling something when I was on the beach looking at the ocean. And the first time I saw a rainbow, I just felt this big thing all through my body. I could feel it; I just couldn't put it into words.

"That's what brought me to the desert. Get away from the noise, the pollution, the people and get closer to God. This is the real world. Very little that's man-made. My faith is strong here because I see God in everything. My religion is in the trees, the cactus, the birds, the animals. And it's a peaceful religion. When I look out at the world and all these factions fighting against each other, I feel like if there is any future for religion, it's going to have to be something that is all-inclusive, something that respects everything and everyone. Kinda like my church here. The church of the desert."

ANNA HUFF *Naturalist. Minister. Texan.*

"I THINK MAYBE THE WORD *RELIGION* OFFENDS SOME PEOPLE."

"THE 11TH CHAPTER OF HEBREWS IS THE 'HALL OF FAITH,' and it starts out by saying that faith is being sure of what you hope for and being certain of that which you cannot see."

Bonnie Hunter is a Christian who practices what she truly believes Jesus taught: tolerance in all things.

"I think maybe the word *religion* offends some people. And in this world today, I understand that feeling. It's as if they think you're holding them to a standard or something. Some people do put up barriers, I think, and the truth is, if we put barriers around what God can do or what God says, we don't have an open mind about what God is capable of. He reveals Himself to me in the way that is comfortable to me, but He may be revealing Himself in millions of other ways to other people. And who are we to judge? I believe there is one God, and I believe He came to earth in the person of His son, Jesus Christ. I believe He is risen again, and I believe He will come again. It isn't important to me whether you believe that or not. It is only important that you believe. The older I get, the deeper my faith gets and the wider my tolerance becomes.

"My sister made a remark one day to a friend who was a Muslim. She said, 'Annette, you're the best Christian I know.' We see goodness that we believe is born of the Holy Spirit in our lives, but then you see people who do not profess to be Christians, and they out-Christian us all.

"There was a man by the name of Jim Elliot who was a missionary to the Auca Indians, and he was killed as a very young man. Before he died, he made this statement: 'He is no fool who gives what he cannot keep to gain what he cannot lose.' That is the reassurance that my faith brings to my life. I am blessed."

BONNIE HUNTER *Christian. Gentle Spirit. Texan.*

"On the long journey of human life,
faith is the best companion."

THE BUDDHA

"GOD WORKS IN MYSTERIOUS WAYS.

IN TEXAS, EVEN THROUGH HORSES."

REVA WILLIAMS HARRIS IS LOUD. IT COMES FROM HER ENERGY. Her fearlessness. Her wisdom. Her faith. It's just her natural way of being excited about whatever she is telling you about.

Ask her about her daughter, though, and she gets soft. Not in a sad way — in a way that tells you she is proud. Reva's daughter Kim contracted encephalitis when she was an infant. It left her partially paralyzed and mentally challenged. When Kim was 15, Reva heard about a place where they used horses to stimulate the mentally and physically challenged, and she took her daughter there. After her fourth ride, Kim got down off the horse and walked. Reva said it was God doing His work through a horse.

"Doctors told me my daughter wouldn't live and that if she did, she'd just be a vegetable. I figured God had other plans. And I was right. Because when I saw what riding that horse could do for her, I realized that God wanted me to help other kids like her. So we raised some money, and we started an equestrian center and therapy petting zoo at the Richmond State School. And it's not just horses. I put a rabbit in the hands of a man who had a stroke. He began petting the rabbit, and his hands — which had been paralyzed by the stroke — began to move, and the color returned to them. I believe that God works His miracles in many ways. We just have to be open to them." Reva is open.

REVA WILLIAMS HARRIS *Miracle Worker. Baptist. Texan.*

"I GO TO THE CHURCH OF NATURE."

"MY HUSBAND AND I LOVE THE OUTDOORS SO MUCH. Friday afternoon I was sitting on the San Saba River with a fishing pole and a line in the river, and that to me is church. Watching the sun go down. Watching the birds fly. Watching the ripple of the river as it goes by. God is there. He is with me, and I don't have to go into a building with an altar to find Him. I think God comes to us in so many different ways, sometimes to warn us. Sometimes to calm us. Sometimes to simply say you're on the wrong path or the right path."

Liz Melton is one of those people you feel you've known for a long time the minute you meet her. She professes to no particular religion, but she has an abiding faith. You can hear it.

"I see signs of God all around me, all the time. Most of the time, they happen when you're not looking for them. All of a sudden, something happens, and you know God's hand is all over it.

"I'll tell you a story. My husband and I were in Costa Rica. We took a tour of a cloud forest with another couple. The facility we chose was totally random, but when we arrived, it was apparent that it was based on spirituality and the belief in God. There were Scriptures and engravings on the rocks throughout our walk and quiet, peaceful rest stops to meditate and pray. We came to a waterfall that was out of the sun, almost no light. But we asked the guide to take our picture with our camera for a souvenir. I remember it was cold, and the mist from the waterfall was swirling. My husband put his arm around me, and the camera clicked. Back home after we had developed the film, there were only two images that were clear and well-lit. In all this darkness, there was the image of the two of us, and way back in the recesses of the cave was the clear and distinct image of a statue that was sitting on a ledge, as if in a halo. It was the Virgin Mary. We couldn't believe it. I took this as a sign that I am where I am supposed to be. I am doing what I am supposed to be doing. And I have God looking over my shoulder at all times."

LIZ MELTON *Church of Nature. Fisherwoman. Texan.*

"Hey...remember Me?"

"I spent a whole lot of years doing what I wanted to do. And I mean, I got to do some pretty cool stuff. I was a cowboy; I was a deputy sheriff. But when I was about 38, 39, the Lord started working on me, saying, 'Hey...remember Me?' So when I was 40, I finally said, 'I surrender — You want me to be a pastor? I surrender, Lord.'"

Mark Sprague is the pastor at High Desert Baptist Church in Marathon, Texas, a town of 550 people just north of Big Bend. A big congregation on Sunday night is maybe eight–12 people.

"I'll be honest with you. There's some days I wake up, and I go, 'I don't know what I'm doing this for.' It's usually Monday morning. You know what they say — preachers always quit on Monday. I'm like, 'How in the world are we going to pay our bills this month?' And then all of a sudden, something comes in from some folks I never met before, and the Lord kind of cracks me in the back of the head and says, 'Now if you'd just listened to Me in the first place; I told you I'd take care of you.'

"And then you get to sit down with a young man who has been in prison twice and has just had a real tough life, and you work on him and you pray with him — and the tears start rolling down his face, and he puts his faith in the Lord. Hey, the bumps in the road that I got to go through — you know what? They're gone. The Lord has a way of, when I start feeling sorry for myself, He says, 'Hey, you remember that guy? You remember the guy you got to lead to the Lord? Hey...it's all worth it.'"

MARK SPRAGUE *Cowboy. Pastor. Texan.*

"I say Allah, you say God.

It's the same."

"When I was growing up, we were one of only two Muslim families in our town, and I remember how accepting my friends were of me. They were interested in how I prayed. It was just a very warm, natural curiosity about me. No hatred. No fear. But things changed after 9/11."

Jilan Bruce is a Sunni Muslim born of a white father from Arizona and an Iranian mother from Tanzania.

"It was very hard to be a Muslim in the Western world for a while. I guess people thought that those men who flew those planes represented Islam. But that couldn't be further from the truth. They represented nothing more than their own hatred. I think the backlash against all Muslims was incredibly unfortunate, but I've noticed, as time has passed, that more people of other religions are reaching out to find out about my faith. And what they're finding is that we all believe in the same God. Just because we say 'Allah' doesn't mean we worship a different God. It just means we have a different language and a different word for God. My faith teaches me to be a good person, to look out for others. My faith teaches me to respect all people. My faith teaches me to love God.

"Isn't that what all faiths teach?"

JILAN BRUCE *Muslim. Human. Texan.*

"The dirtiest word in the
English language is *they*."

"A TV show is 30 minutes, but when you take out the commercials, it's about 20. People are programmed to listen for maybe 20 minutes. So I tell young preachers, 'You speak for 18 minutes. Your job is speaking. Their job is listening. They're gonna finish their job at 18 minutes whether you're finished or not.'"

Gerald Mann founded Riverbend Church 27 years ago. He's retired now and battling Parkinson's disease, but it hasn't affected his charm or his sense of humor.

"When I was 40, I decided I really didn't fit into the church I grew up with, so I decided to build a church that I would have really liked when I was young, a church built on the foundation of inclusiveness. I think the dirtiest word in the English language is *they*. People would ask me, 'What is your policy on "them"?' And I would say, 'We don't have a policy.' I believe that the main enemy in all the world's religions, whether it's Islam or theism or Christianity, is arrogance. Nobody has a curb on God.

"I don't think that, through prayer, you can convince God to do something for you that He doesn't want to do. I think prayer is a way to change yourself. So I don't ever say, 'God, change the world to fit me.' I say, 'Change me to fit the world.'

"I think the thing I enjoyed most about my job was watching little-hearted people become big-hearted people. I don't know if I had much to do with that, but I do think we created an atmosphere that allowed that to happen. I'm pretty proud of that."

GERALD MANN   *Christian. Retired Minister. Texan.*

"IT HAS NEVER BEEN MORE CLEAR

THAT WE ARE ALL IN THIS TOGETHER."

"I AM A CHRISTIAN, AND I FEEL THAT MY CHRISTIANITY is enriched by the study of other faith traditions and by interaction with people of other faiths. When I see the devotion of a Muslim and the passion of a Jew, I look to my own tradition and say, 'Where do I feel those things?' I ask myself, 'How does my own tradition call me to deeper levels of commitment that I had not expected of myself?'"

Reverend Emilee Dawn Whitehurst is an ordained Presbyterian minister and the executive director of AAIM (Austin Area Interreligious Ministries).

"I have this deep hope that the commonalities unite us more than the differences divide us. So how do we find what unites us? We have to do the work of caring and listening and hearing so that people don't feel like they have to put what they are most passionate about aside to be in a room together. I like to think that all the religious traditions are wisdom traditions for all of humankind. We've all seen the hurt that can be caused in the name of religion; we have seen the wars and the violence and the hatred, but I want people to understand that the wisdom of the Koran belongs to everybody. And the Torah speaks to everyone, and certainly the Christian Testament doesn't belong to Christians alone. There are vital resources in all spiritual traditions for us as we face global problems. And it has never been more clear that we are all in this together."

EMILEE DAWN WHITEHURST *Presbyterian. Voice of Reason. Texan.*

"THIS IS COMMON GROUND.

AND WE ARE BLESSED TO BE HERE."

"WE WERE BLESSED BEYOND OUR WILDEST DREAMS, and we asked ourselves what we could do that might make a difference in the world somehow. What could we do responsibly with what we've been given?"

Ken and Joyce Beck took the good fortune that came to them through the success of Dell Computer and listened to their hearts.

"Our friends asked us, 'If you could do anything in the world, without restriction, what would it be? What would you do?' The answer was, 'We would create a spiritual destination. A place where individuals, groups and companies could come and explore their spirituality. A place where we can expand our awareness of who we are.' The Crossings is a place that celebrates the fact that we are all one. Each year The Crossings celebrates unity between the different faiths in a conference called 'Common Ground.'

"There are all these religions in the world, and we are all worshiping in different ways. We may worship a different deity or use a different name, but in the end, we believe that we are all connected to that same supreme being. The Crossings celebrates inclusivity. As you walk to our sanctuary, you will see the symbols of the seven major religions of the world because we want you to leave behind the separateness when you come here. This is common ground. And we are blessed to be here."

KEN & JOYCE BECK *Humanitarians. Christians. Texans.*

"I'M PRETTY SURE THIS IS HOW
GOD WOULD HAVE US BE."

"I WAS ATTENDING TILLOTSON COLLEGE IN 1941 when I decided to marry. Now I was raised a Presbyterian, but there were no colored Presbyterian churches in Austin at the time [churches were segregated in those days]. I told my history teacher about my dilemma, and she said, 'That's okay; I'm getting a group of people together to start an Episcopal church. Why don't you join us?' So I did."

Bertha Sadler Means is one of the founding members of St. James Episcopal Church in Austin. It is regarded by many as one of the most racially, socioeconomically diverse churches in the nation.

"I am the granddaughter of a former slave from Tennessee who founded the first colored Cumberland Presbyterian church in Texas. I pretty much came up not looking at the color of somebody's skin. I see people as people. Not white people. Not black people. Not gay people. Just people. I'm pretty sure this is how God would have us be. But I vividly remember segregation, and I remember the separate toilets and the separate water fountains and such. Those were turbulent times, and we had to rely on God to carry us through. I suppose that is one of the reasons why our church was so important to us — because it was a haven of compassion and love. We consciously extended ourselves to make it as diverse as we could possibly make it. We live the Golden Rule. We welcome everybody. Would you like to come to our church?"

BERTHA SADLER MEANS *Episcopalian. Colorblind. Texan.*

"WE HAVE BEEN PUT HERE BY GOD, AND WE HAVE AN INNATE KNOWLEDGE ABOUT HOW WE SHOULD LIVE."

"IT SEEMS TO ME THAT WHAT THE CREATOR HAS INTENDED is that we live by the Golden Rule, in proper relationship with each other. What we struggle with during our whole human existence is learning how to live in relationship with each other and with the created order of everything around us."

Garland Robertson is a man of peace. He flew planes in Vietnam, and that experience led him to the belief that war is never the answer. He was drawn to the Mennonite faith because of its historical position of peace.

"We oftentimes create our own pattern of living and draw circles around it, leaving some people outside. Jesus tended to move the boundaries outward, and His example teaches us to just keep moving those boundaries out until the whole created order is included in them.

"Faith is the pursuit of living in accord with the spiritual wisdom that arises from within the human spirit. We have been put here by God, and we have an innate knowledge about how we should live among other living things. Faith is acknowledging that wisdom and ordering our lives according to it, trusting that the Creator had intention and purpose in that design. Trusting that we should not force our own opinions and positions on others, but rather try to create opportunities for dialogue so we can understand what their concerns are, what their fears are. If we can do that, then there is a way for us to start to resolve conflicts between us."

GARLAND ROBERTSON   *Mennonite. Peace Activist. Texan.*

"I think Jesus looks at us today
and says, 'What did you miss in what
I said about loving one another?'"

EVELYN ROMIG
DEAN OF THE SCHOOL OF HUMANITIES
HOWARD PAYNE UNIVERSITY

"I try to see God in everyone."

"My exposure to religion when I was a child consisted of my mother dumping me off at Sunday school and my father picking me up. I wouldn't say I was exactly steeped in Christianity."

Carlisle Vandervoort has been meditating for 18 years. She will tell you that she began to see the benefit of it when animals started being attracted to her.

"I'm serious. After about eight years of meditating, I began to feel my heart change. And I noticed that my relationship with animals was different. They began approaching me and that rarely happened before. What I realized was that it was what was going on inside me that they were drawn to. I had begun to see God within me. And they did, too.

"Now I try to see God in everyone. And that's a real test sometimes. Because I find myself judging the people who judge me for my beliefs or way of life, and I have to stop and step back and ask myself, 'Where am I scared?' Because basically my fear is that they're going to shove me into a corner and not recognize me. So I have to ask myself, 'Where am I not recognizing them?' It's very easy to become spiritually self-righteous. And that is the biggest reason for division in the world today. Hey, it's okay to have different belief systems, as long as some form of the Golden Rule is part of that belief system."

CARLISLE VANDERVOORT *Hindu. Seeker. Texan.*

"Y'ALL LOOK AROUND — THIS IS WHAT HEAVEN LOOKS LIKE."

"WE ALL HAVE THE SAME REVELATION. We all share the same Lord. He's the reason any of us are getting in, and since He's going to let plenty of people in that we don't know anything about, we better start learning how to get along down here so that we're not in for a big surprise up there."

Leroy Behnke speaks with the voice of a man who is used to telling it like it is. Leroy's a Catholic, but he's a lover of all things God.

"A friend of mine died a few years back. Harold Moore was the minister of the Church of Christ. Now the Church of Christ was a pretty small church at the time, and Harold had lots of friends. So the pastor of the First Baptist Church, the biggest church in Shallowater, called Harold's wife and offered to have his service there. And I'm giving a eulogy at this fine man's funeral. I'm standing up there, a Catholic, at a pulpit in a Baptist church, speaking at the funeral of a Church of Christ minister. I looked out at the congregation and said, 'Y'all look around — this is what heaven looks like.' There were people of all colors, young and old, Catholics, Methodists, Baptists, Church of Christ, everybody. It was absolutely uncontroversial. It was the Golden Rule in action. Deep in our hearts, we know that that's the way it's supposed to be. You can see the fingerprints of God all over this."

LEROY BEHNKE   *Small-town Boy. Big-time Heart. Texan.*

3.

COMMON GROUND
FOUND IN VALUES

Compassion, Charity, Humility and Forgiveness

"It is not so much what you believe in that matters, as the way in which you believe it and proceed to translate that belief into actions."

DR. LIN YUTANG, CHINESE WRITER AND TRANSLATOR

"Until we look at life from the bottom up, we never really know what compassion is."

"Jesus, in the 13th chapter of John's Gospel, is washing the feet of the apostles before He dies. He says, 'Do you understand what I am doing?' He was washing their feet, the closest things to the earth. Jesus is telling us that Christianity is a theology from the bottom up. The same thing is applicable in Luke's story of the Good Samaritan. The Good Samaritan didn't pass up the guy in the ditch because he knew what it was like to be in the ditch. He wasn't looking at life from the top down. He was looking at life from the bottom up."

Father Milam Joseph was ordained in 1964 after graduating from Notre Dame. He was a pastor for 21 years and the president of the University of Dallas for eight. He is presently the Episcopal Vicar to the Bishop of the Roman Catholic Diocese of Dallas.

"The concept of compassion is what the gospel is all about. It's really what God is all about. It's about making up what is lacking in others, and we make up what is lacking in others when they can't do it for themselves. The common ground for all religions has to be, in my opinion, the challenge of caring for, being sensitive to, the disenfranchised of society. Jesus never really talked a lot about religion. There wasn't any dogmatic presentation. In His final volley in Matthew 25, He didn't talk about religion at all. He talked about what you did to the least of these, you did to Me. That is the common ground."

FATHER MILAM JOSEPH *Catholic Priest. Good Samaritan. Texan.*

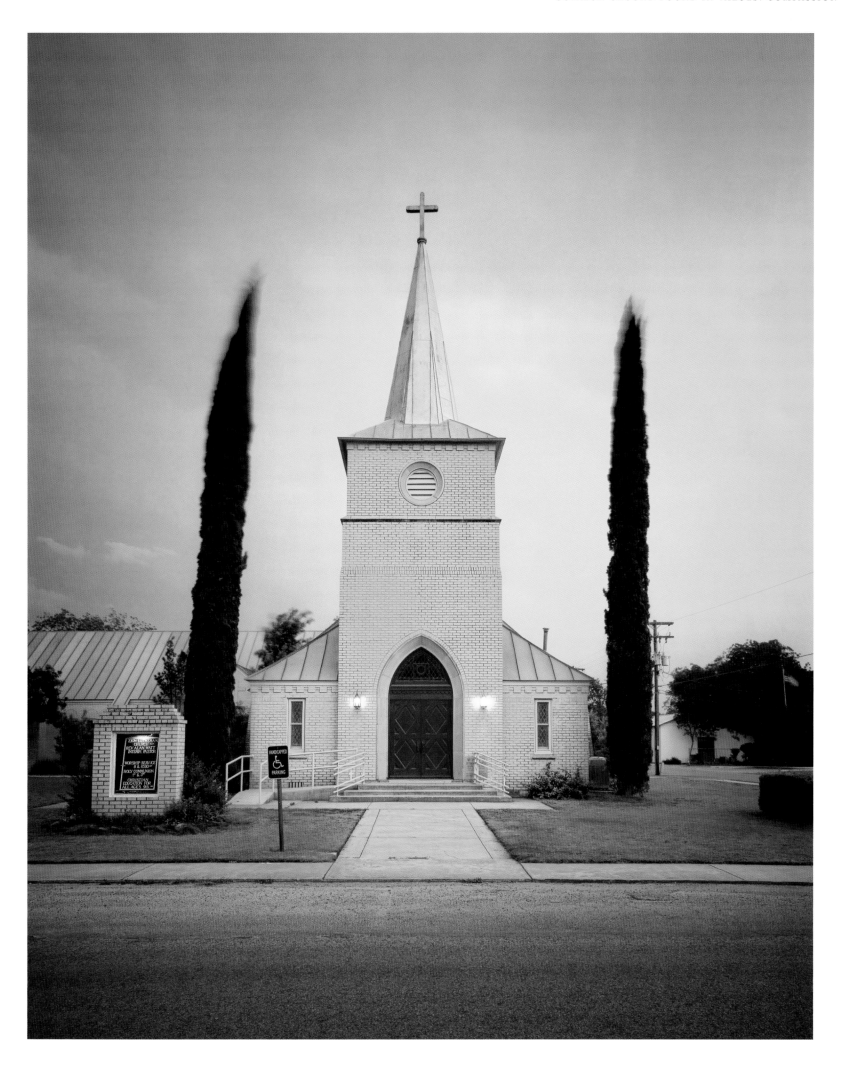

"God is in us and we are in God."

"People tell me that my garden is my church. They step into the garden, and they feel that same sense of investment and symbolism that many other people feel in churches. I feel them in both places. I rarely step into a place of worship, no matter how humble or what faith tradition, that I don't get a sense that this is an expression of awe and gratitude. And people feel permission when they step through those doors, in a way they don't in their ordinary lives, to let the mind contemplate the mystery of creation."

Tom Spencer is a man who believes that the garden is not only a place to explore nature, but also a place to explore God.

"There is a Buddhist way of saying that compassion is the fruit of humility. It's the virtue that grows within us when we look at the world realistically and humbly and with gratitude. We develop the sense of concerned, loving care for those around us, and I think compassion has to extend beyond just the circle of humanity. I believe that God is in us, and we are in God, and all of creation is the same. God has a thousand, ten thousand voices. You can hear it in the birds. You can see it in the streets in the morning when parents are walking with their kids or perhaps an older woman is walking with a companion. That is something incredibly beautiful, and you have to see God in those things. And once you begin to see God in creation and each other, that spark of the divine, how could you not feel compassion? And all of the great faith traditions dwell on that and try to drive us toward it. One of the great strengths of the Christian and Jewish traditions is that focus on how we live together. And the answer is, with compassion."

TOM SPENCER *Gardener. Buddhist. Texan.*

"I'VE ALWAYS VIEWED
THE FAITH COMMUNITY MORE
LIKE A SUPPORT GROUP."

"THAT WAS NEVER MORE EVIDENT than in the aftermath of Hurricane Katrina when Houston opened its arms to thousands of evacuees. When we are at our best, we are willing to make sacrifices for others — no matter who they are, no matter where they are from — and to rejoice in the sacrifices because it's the way to repay the gift of life."

Bill White is the mayor of Houston. He will tell you that Matthew 25 has always had significance for him but never so dramatically than in the days and weeks after Katrina.

"'When I was hungry, you fed Me. When I was thirsty, you gave Me drink. When I was a stranger, you took Me in.' I can't tell you how many times this Scripture came to me as we worked in the long days after Katrina. We had never dealt with anything like this before. No one has. But I learned that when you ask people to do things — appealing to their deepest values — they will respond in extraordinary ways. I cannot express how important the different faith communities were to this amazing effort.

"In every faith tradition, you'll find people who base their lives on the simple principles that the world isn't about you, that life is a gift, that there is beautiful mystery to how we got here and what will come after. We can express our gratitude and our hope by caring for our fellow human beings. There is so much we have in common. And I am proud to have been a witness to mankind at its best."

BILL WHITE *Mayor. Methodist. Texan.*

"I HAVE GREAT COMPASSION FOR

PEOPLE WHO HAVE NO FAITH."

"I AM A CHRISTIAN BECAUSE THAT IS WHAT I KNOW. But it would be inconsistent of me to think about a loving God and a compassionate Christ that would bar from heaven faithful people of other traditions. What is it? 'In my Father's house, there are many rooms.' I think we have much to learn from people of other faiths. It is my belief that we all share the same God."

Liz Stewart will tell you that she was mostly "unchurched" growing up, but she will tell you that God and her relationship with Jesus have been at the center of her life since just before the birth of her third child, Grace.

"I think in the end, God expects one thing of us: to live every moment as generously and compassionately as possible. Look for opportunities to help. Look for people to encourage. To me that is the main job of a church — to remind us to lift each other up. To take every opportunity we can to perform acts of love and service. That's what my faith means to me. I have great compassion for people who have no faith. When I think of 9/11 or when I think of Katrina and all the other tragedies in the world, and I hear someone say, 'How could God let that happen?' I am comforted by the reminder that God is not in the act; rather He is in the rubble. He is there to help us when times are tough. I am strengthened by my faith."

LIZ STEWART *Mother. Christian. Texan.*

"I was hungry and you gave me food, I was thirsty and you gave me drink,
I was a stranger and you welcomed me.... Truly I say to you,
as you did it to one of the least of these my brothers, you did it to me."

MATTHEW 25:35, 40, ESV

"LIFE IS A FREEWAY TO GOD. THERE ARE OFF-RAMPS ON THIS FREEWAY, BUT FORTUNATELY, THERE ARE ALSO ON-RAMPS. GOD ALWAYS SHOWS US WAYS TO FIND OUR WAY BACK TO HIM."

"I'VE TAKEN A LOT OF WRONG EXITS IN MY LIFE, but it just seems like God's always ahead — I mean very close ahead, making more and more on-ramps. He says, 'Okay, that didn't work. I had this great plan for your life. I wish you'd followed it, but okay, we've got another plan here.'"

Bob Decker is a Houston policeman who, four years ago, made a wrong turn in a Mexican border town and discovered God's latest plan for him. He named it Paper Houses Across the Border. Because that is what thousands of people along the border in Mexico live in. They are the people who work in factories for as little as $39 a week and try as hard as they can to survive. They have nothing but faith. And Bob Decker.

"As I drove back from Mexico that first time, I couldn't get it out of my head. I argued with God a lot on that drive: 'Why don't You do something for these people? Why do You let them live this way?' I guess the answer was, 'That's why you took the wrong turn. I just built you an on-ramp.' The first time I went back, I bought stuff to make sandwiches and some used clothing and started giving it away. From there the mission has taken off. The Houston Police Department helped me set up a nonprofit and began raising money. Churches of all faiths have contributed. The response has been almost overwhelming. But we've managed to help these people in ways that are so small to us but so big to them, and maybe more importantly, we are seeing people here give us their time, their money and their hearts to help people they don't know. And that is what compassion is. That is what God would have us do. What is it in Matthew 25: I tell you the truth, whatever you did for one of the least of these brothers of Mine, you did for Me. All I know is when I'm down there working with these people, I feel like I am walking with Christ next to me. I have never felt the love I feel when I'm on a Paper Houses mission."

BOB DECKER *Policeman. Christian. Texan.*

"CHARITY IS GIVING UP YOUR TORTILLA, HONEY, WHEN IT'S THE ONLY ONE."

"IT IS A PRIVILEGE TO WORK WITH THE POOR because they have no facade. They only have their faith."

Lydia Hernandez runs Manos de Cristo. It is a place where the poor in the Mexican community can come for help for clothes, for food, for medicine, for love. Lydia knows about love. And she knows about the plight of the poor.

"I think that the real purpose of Manos de Cristo is to live with and among the poor so we can experience Christ among us. While it is for us to reach out to those who don't have, it is as much for those who don't have to reach out to us.

"We were so poor when I was a kid, and my dad would always be bringing people home to share our dinner. I remember there would sometimes be only enough dough that my mother could only make one tortilla apiece for us, and we would hide our tortillas under our plates. My dad would pray, 'Heavenly Father, we are so grateful to You for everything You give us, everything that is hot and tasty and good. And, God, I just give You thanks because I know that there is somebody at this table who, out of the generosity of their heart, is going to be sharing with this man that I have brought home. Thank You, Jesus. Amen.' We'd be pinching each other like, who is going to give up their tortilla? My dad's praying and we're fighting about it. So charity is giving up your tortilla, honey, when it's the only one.

"It's a big step just to acknowledge that there is something greater than all of us looking out for all of us. That is the common ground of all religions."

LYDIA HERNANDEZ *Presbyterian. Angel. Texan.*

"WHEN YOU ARE WITH THE DYING, YOU ARE IN THE DIVINE PRESENCE OF GOD."

"I WAS DIAGNOSED IN 1991, AND IN THE YEARS SINCE, I have realized that God is so much bigger than I ever had any idea of. That can be scary at first. But then it's just completely liberating. It has taken me to places in my heart that I never dreamed of going."

David Smith is HIV positive. He is also one of the most caring, loving, giving, full-of-life people you will ever meet.

"I am the director of the Hill Country Ride for AIDS, and I work with many of the organizations that the Ride benefits. One of the things I am blessed to be able to do is to take meals to people with AIDS who would otherwise go hungry. And in the process of delivering these meals, I saw that what I was doing was so much more than delivering a meal. For most of them, I am probably their only personal contact all day, and I can see the incredible power of the human spirit in each of them.

"I remember one delivery in particular. It was in an apartment complex I was a little bit nervous about entering. I knocked on the door, and I could tell someone was in there — but it took maybe five minutes for someone to reach the door. And this man with the most beautiful smile, the kind of smile that you can tell is coming from within, opened the door. He was so happy to see me and so happy to see this meal, and he had neuropathy — extreme debilitating pain in his feet — and it took him that long to reach the door. I looked at this person who had nothing, who was probably dying of his disease, and I only saw joy.

"I also work with hospices, and I am in the presence of many people who pass over. And I have to tell you, every one of these experiences is what I would say is the closest I've ever been to a real divine presence of God. I have not witnessed a single passing that the person, at the very end, wasn't experiencing the most awesome peace. And each of them, in his or her own unique way, was telling us this is beautiful. What a gift."

DAVID SMITH   *Methodist. Caregiver. Texan.*

"God loves me unconditionally, and I don't question His taste."

"My nephew says that I work in an alley and give out food to people and talk to drunks."

Sister Mary William, D.C., is Irish, outspoken and a Daughter of Charity at St. Mary's Cathedral in downtown Austin.

"We're a downtown church, so we have many homeless people and people who need assistance. America is just beginning to realize that we have poor people in our country. But part of it is that we've become so materialistic that we measure success by material things, and the people who come to us for service have a closeness to God because that is their only strength. They don't see what they don't have as a failure. They see it as a challenge. And they don't blame God for what they don't have. And that's faith. That's real faith. They have taught me what it means to be poor of spirit. You know, the first Beatitude is, 'Blessed are the poor in spirit, for theirs is the kingdom of heaven.' The poor teach me what it is to be rich in spirit.

"A relationship with God is a growing thing. It is ever ancient, ever new. The relationship with God must be cultivated, just like a relationship with a friend. That leads you to what religion, what community, expresses God best for you.

"God loves me unconditionally, and I don't question His taste."

SISTER MARY WILLIAM, D.C. *Catholic. Irish. Texan.*

"I KNEEL, YOU STAND. I FOLD MY HANDS, YOU PUT THEM OUT. WE'RE DOING THE SAME THING."

"CHARITY IS A GIFT TO US. It is God saying, 'Here is your chance to be an angel today. Here is your chance to give someone something they really need.' And what they may really need is just for someone to look them in the eye and smile instead of looking upon them with pity. Someone to listen. Someone to care. That is charity. Through those people, God is saying, 'I am right here. You don't have to look any further.' You never know when God's going to say, 'Hello! Time out! I'm up here. You're not in charge; you don't have control over your life. I do.'"

Bianca Aguilar is an angel every day as she opens the doors of Casa Marianella and helps the migrants who have no one else to turn to. It is a place to stay. A place to eat. A place where someone listens.

"We're just humans. We're looking for the same thing. We're just trying to make it in this world the same way as everybody else. To me everybody believes in the same thing. It's just worded differently. I kneel, you stand. I fold my hands, you put them out. It's just variations, just like there are variations in race and variations in language. They're doing the same thing we are. They're probably praying to the same God we are. They believe in forgiveness. They believe in love. They all want peace. How much more do we want to divide ourselves in this world? How much more do we want to isolate who we are when we're all reaching for the same thing?"

BIANCA AGUILAR *Catholic. Angel. Texan.*

"Humility always radiates the greatness and glory of God.
Through humility we grow in love. Humility is the beginning of sanctity."

MOTHER TERESA

"GOD IS IN PRISON AND HE'LL NEVER GET OUT. BECAUSE THERE'S TOO MUCH WORK FOR HIM TO DO THERE."

"I WAS SITTING IN PRISON, A VERY ANGRY MAN. It was a combination of 20 years of alcohol and drug use, and I had come to my bottom. I was at the point where there was no solution other than to cry out for something outside of myself that would relieve me of the insanity I was living."

David Peña heard the call in a prison cell, the day before he was planning to kill another inmate.

"I remember I was sick that day and had to go to the infirmary. While I was sitting there, they brought in a man shackled from head to toe. Shirtless, no shoes, covered from head to toe with tattoos — so many you didn't know whether to look at him or read him. We got to talking, and he asked me what year it was. I said, 'Man, how long you been in here...don't even know what year it is.' As we waited, he told me his story. He had been in prison for 26 years, most of them in solitary. He said he came in on a 10-year sentence but killed two inmates and got two life terms on top of his 10 years. Here was this man, in prison for life and still full of himself. Cocky, arrogant, thinking he was on top of the world. I looked at this man and I saw myself, and I just started shaking. I left the infirmary, went back to my cell and fell down on my knees. I said, 'God, I don't know who You are, but if You care anything about me, You'll show me the way out of here. I can't live this way anymore.'"

Today David has a degree in psychology and runs an outreach program for ex-cons.

DAVID PEÑA *Ex-con. Christian Minister. Texan.*

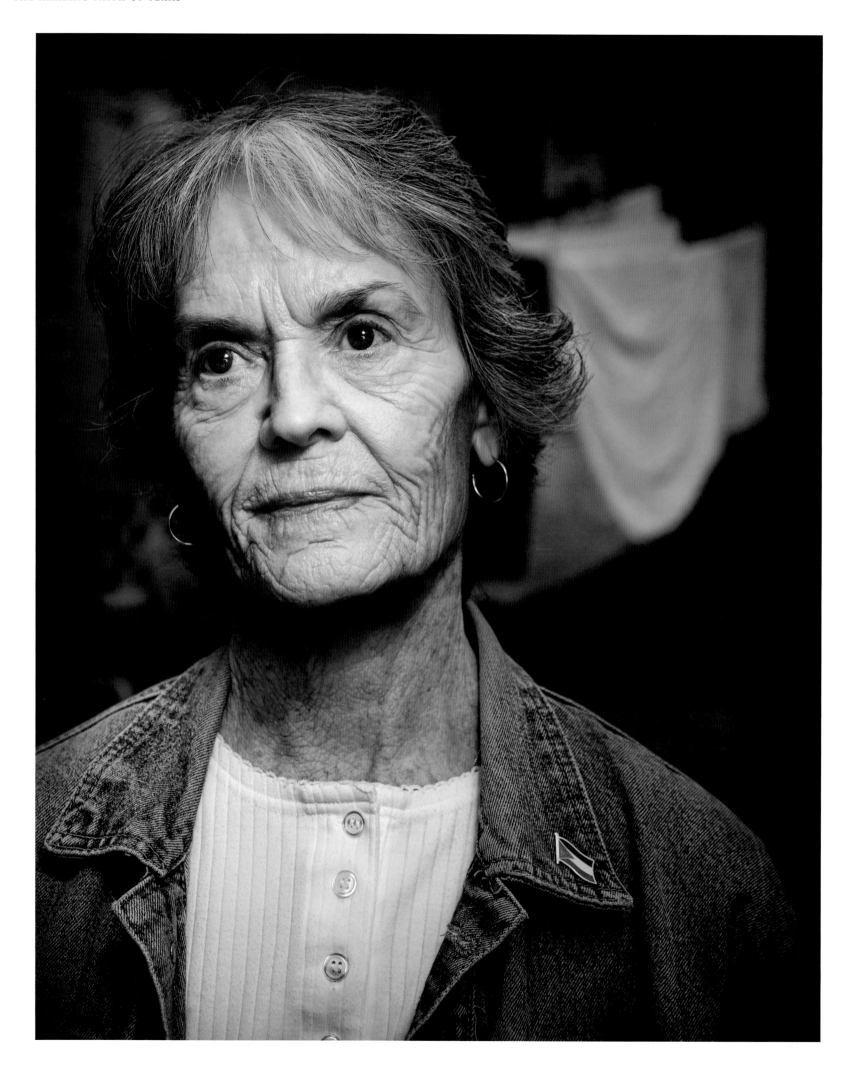

"We need to always be able to step back and say, 'There might be another way of thinking than mine.'"

"I don't know how we can come together and have reconciliation and find that common ground unless we come with the humility that none of us is better than any of us."

Carol C. Walker has the look of someone you'd expect to step out of a John Wayne movie. She's a lady with the air of Texas about her, even if you don't know what a Texan is supposed to look like. She's windblown, lean, her face lined by good years in the Texas sun. But it wasn't her years in Texas that brought us to her door. It was her years as a Methodist missionary — to Uruguay, Peru, China and Beirut — that interested us.

"It was an interesting time for me, an interesting time in the world. I was in Beirut when the fighting began there over religion. I went to China in the spring of 1989. I was teaching at a university in Mien-ching when the student demonstrations began in all the big cities. My students kept begging me to march with them, and I kept telling them that it would not be proper. Every day they would march by my window and ask me to join them, and every day I would politely refuse. One day I looked out, and they were carrying a banner that said, 'The teachers support the students,' and once again they asked me to join them. I said, 'Oh, God, don't make me do this' — but you have to listen sometimes, and the call was too great, so I went down and joined the march. I walked with them for about six blocks before I decided that this was something I shouldn't be doing. I bade them farewell and returned to campus. One week later, some of these kids were killed in the Tiananmen Square massacre.

"The day I was leaving China, a student came up to me and asked if he could speak to me alone. He closed the door and said, 'I want you to know that I am religious, too, but I have to keep it secret here.' How fortunate we are here to be able to worship as we choose. We need to always be able to step back and say, 'There might be another way of thinking than mine.'"

CAROL C. WALKER, Ph.D.   *Missionary. Humanitarian. Texan.*

"RELIGION IS FOR INDIVIDUALS.
GOD IS FOR THE WHOLE WORLD."

"WHEN I WAS A KID, MY PARENTS TOOK ME TO AN EPISCOPAL CHURCH, and then we went to a Methodist church and then another and another. And I began to think, 'Why are we moving from one church to another? We're all worshiping the same God, so why are there so many different policies?'"

Dash Crofts speaks with the wisdom of someone who has lived on both sides of life, tasted the successes, the excesses, the cheers and the doubts. One half of Seals & Crofts, one of the great pop duos in history, Dash is a Bahá'í.

"I went through periods in my life where I felt like I had lost my way and that I didn't want to be Dash Crofts anymore. I didn't want to be a rock star. I just wanted to be a normal human being like everybody else and find out what it's like to live like them. So I would take off on my remoteness from God, and then about two or three years into it, I'm thinking, 'What am I doing?' You don't see outside of those blinders; you're satisfying yourself and your ego and all the other things, but you're forgetting what reality is. Boy, it hit me like a ton of bricks when I came back from that. I asked everybody for forgiveness, especially God.

"Religion is a personal thing. It's between you and God. You get to the next world, and you open your suitcase and realize it's empty. Oh my gosh, I didn't bring what I need. I'm packin' my suitcase for the next world, you know."

DASH CROFTS *Entertainer. Bahá'í. Texan.*

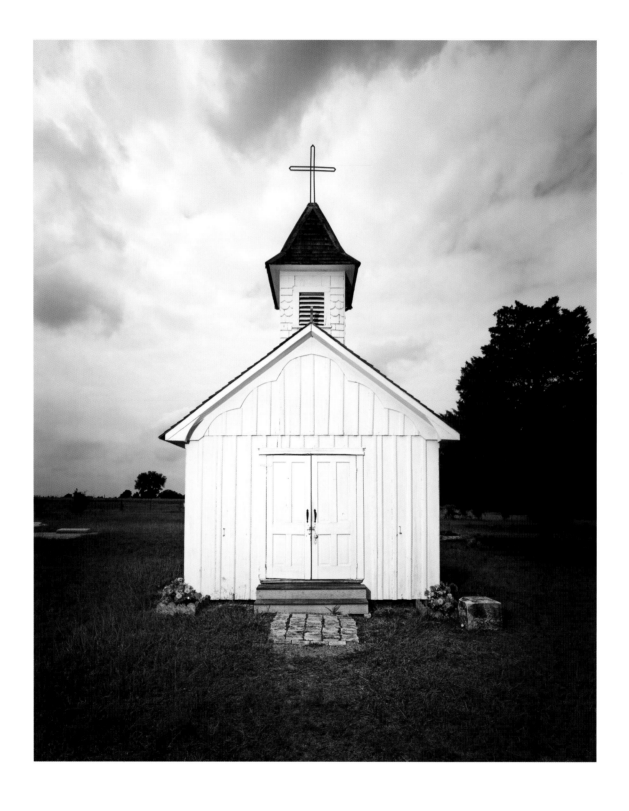

"Mommy, God told me
to tell you that She's a man."

"I CONSTANTLY ASK MY CHILDREN, 'Where were you before you came through me? What were you doing? Tell me about that place. Do you remember any of it?' I remember lying on the bed with my daughter Lilly when she was maybe 18 months old. We were talking, and I asked her, 'How did you get so wise?' She smiled and pointed at the spot on her forehead between her eyes. The Buddhists call that the third eye, or the eye of God. I just felt a chill."

Sara Hickman is a singer/songwriter by profession. Her smile radiates the light of God. Her music speaks of the joys of life.

"A woman I know noticed her son, who was four at the time, sometimes carrying on animated conversations with someone who wasn't there. She asked him who he was talking to, and he said, 'God.' She said, 'Would you mind asking God for me if God is a man or a woman?' The boy said, 'Sure' and went off and had his little conversation. He came back and said, 'Mommy, God told me to tell you that She's a man.' That sort of wisdom answers every question you could ever have about God. That God is everything we could ever hope for God to be. I think children are the messengers of God. They are the angels among us, and if we are humble and just listen, we can learn from them.

"In 1981 there was a plane crash in the Potomac River in Washington. There was one man in that freezing water that day who swam around and passed the rope from the helicopter to other people instead of taking the rope himself. He saved five people before he died. This man gave the ultimate sacrifice to live out his compassion for other people. He gave his life for the lives of others. The question is, what would I have done in his place? I like to think I would have done the same.

"I think God wants us to explore our relationship with the world, our relationship with Him/Her. And the greatest job of faith-filled people is to see the faith and the God and the love in other people."

SARA HICKMAN *Singer. Mother. Methodist. Texan.*

"The journey to God is about us. Not I."

"When I was a kid, we would go to church on Sunday. We would sit there and listen to the sermon, and then we would get up and go, everyone saying to each other, 'See ya next Sunday.'"

Tim Cook is the minister of the Church of Conscious Harmony, a Christian Contemplative community in Austin. He is a Christian. He is, however, a student of all things spiritual. And if you talk to him for a few minutes, you will find yourself becoming interested in all things spiritual.

"When I grew up, I became a pastor at a church with a pulpit and a choir and a congregation, and I stood up on Sunday and preached a sermon, and then we all said, 'See ya next Sunday.' I never lost the feeling that I wanted to share my spiritual journey more than just one hour a week. We decided to try an experiment. Would it be possible to create a monastery without walls? Would it be possible to create a contemplative community that extended into our homes with daily devotional practices and an awareness of togetherness? We had two questions: Can 20th-century Christians make God the center of our lives, and can we find people of like minds to share the journey?

"The answer to both was yes! The Apostle Paul called us to be transformed by the renewing of our minds, and we only really know that is happening in a community by how we feel and act toward each other. So now instead of standing at a pulpit and preaching to a congregation, I sit in a chair and share my spiritual journey with friends. Yes, it's a church and I am a minister. But for us it's a collaborative journey. And every time we stand and join hands to sing or pray, I never feel my own heart beating until I feel the pulse between our touching palms. But more importantly, I then become aware of the heartbeats of every person in the room. A community of people reaching deeply into our Christian roots, all religions and spiritual traditions for insight, wisdom and inspiration. Because we have to come with the humility that we can't do it alone."

TIM COOK *Minister. Christian Contemplative. Texan.*

"To err is human, to forgive, divine."

ALEXANDER POPE

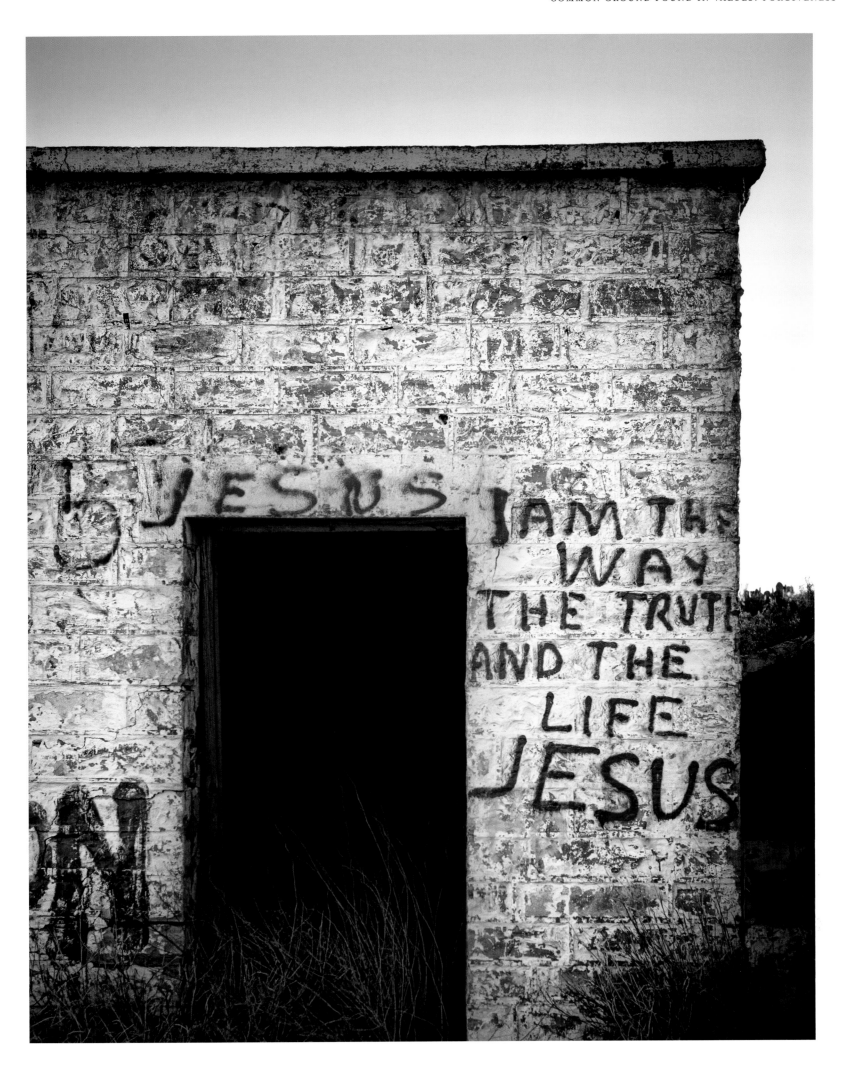

"FORGIVENESS IS GOD'S WAY
OF TEACHING YOU LOVE."

"MY YOUNGEST SON, GABRIEL, NEARLY DROWNED WHEN HE WAS TWO. We were at a pool one summer day, I was reading and he was playing close to me. There were many children at the pool that day, all playing.... 'Mommy, Mommy, Mommy, look at this.' It was just a cacophony of voices out there."

Aniela Maree Costello is one of those people who seem to be in the presence of God at all times. She says her goal every morning is to love and love well. Love impulsively. Love mindfully. She will tell you she learned that from her son.

"I'm watching my other two children play, and I look beside me where Gabriel has been playing, and I don't see him. I figure he's doing what he's done a thousand times before. He would walk around the pool house, playing this game of hide-and-seek, which we had done numerous times. I would say, 'Gabriel, where are you?' And he'd giggle, and I'd say, 'Gabriel, where are you?' This time I don't hear his laugh, so I walk around, looking and calling him — and then my heart seizes. I scream at the top of my lungs. I have a horrible feeling and run back toward the pool, watching as a woman pulls Gabriel up from the bottom of the pool by his hair. She's a cardiac nurse and she's working on him, and I'm screaming, 'I'm sorry...I'm sorry.' I don't even know what I'm screaming anymore. He's not breathing; he has no pulse. She keeps working, and suddenly, he coughs and opens his eyes.

"One day months later, we're all at the dinner table, and Gabriel interjects something. It is quiet for a moment because he has been inordinately quiet as of late. I ask, 'What's wrong, honey?' He says, 'Mommy, I forgive you.' I say, 'Gabriel, forgive me for what?' He says, 'For drowning me.' And I say, 'I drowned you?' And he says, 'Yes.' I say, 'Honey, how did I drown you?' He says, 'I don't know, but you said I'm sorry, and we only say we're sorry when we've done something wrong.' He was clinically dead, and he was 'watching' me scream 'I'm sorry.' In that instant, I suddenly knew what pure love is. If Gabriel could forgive me for what he thought might have been an intentional drowning, then I can forgive anything of anyone. And I thought, 'This is the kind of love I want for me.' Given to us by a two-year-old boy in one fateful moment."

ANIELA MAREE COSTELLO *Mother. Bahá'í. Texan.*

"GOD IS JUST LOOKIN' FOR PEOPLE TO STAND UP FOR HIM. I'M STANDIN' UP FOR HIM."

"I WAS ROPIN' BACK WHEN THEY DIDN'T LET BLACK FOLKS RODEO with white folks. But then they started lettin' us compete, and I won me three world championships. I remember ridin' in rodeos in those days, and folks would be hollerin' names at me. You know what names I'm talkin' about. But it never did bother me because I was there for a different purpose. I know they wasn't speakin' from their heart. It was just the way they was taught."

Lawrence Coffee smiles like a man who is comfortable in his own skin. Like a man who is satisfied with how he has lived his life. Like a man who is pleased with his relationship with God.

"I'm a deacon here in the Mount Horeb Baptist Church. Been a church here since 1867. Started by a freed slave. We got about eight members now. But you know what? It don't matter how big a church is. God lives in those big churches in Houston and Dallas, and He lives in this little church right here. We're proud of what we have here. I think God is, too."

Next time you're headin' north on Highway 165 to Blanco, look for the little sign for the little church where God lives and stop in and say howdy to Lawrence. He might be out shoeing a horse somewhere, but he'll be right back.

LAWRENCE COFFEE *Cowboy. Baptist. Texan.*

"I CAN FORGIVE YOU; NOW YOU MUST GO ASK GOD FOR FORGIVENESS."

"I USED TO GO TO CHURCH, but it felt empty to me because it was mostly about who had the nicest car and the best diamond rings, and I said, 'God, this is not what I want.' Because in my opinion, God wants your heart, not your clothes. So my church is everywhere."

Lesly Mendez runs a small Mexican curio shop in Marathon, Texas. She is a proud woman who carries herself with the strength of a survivor, someone who has seen the worst that life can serve up and lived to move on. Lesly came to Texas 11 years ago from Honduras with her daughters, one and four at the time. She left her country after her husband was murdered, at her home, in front of her. Time seems to have healed the wound, so we asked her if she had found it in her heart to forgive the man who did this.

"I never thought I would see that man again, but a year after my husband's death, I was on a bus coming from the passport office. This was just days before we moved to America. An accident happened right in front of the bus, and I am a nurse so I got off the bus to see if I could help. I approached the car, and a man, gravely injured, was lying there. He looked up, and to my shock, I realized it was the man who had killed my husband. He recognized me as well. He held out his hand and asked me if I would please forgive him. I took his hand and said, 'Of course I will...but now you must go ask for God's forgiveness'...and he died."

LESLY MENDEZ *Survivor. Believer. Texan.*

"We are from different religions, but we are all from
one source. And we are going to the same place."

Paramahansa Yogananda

The Photographs

Mike Blair

MIKE BLAIR

Mike Blair is executive vice president, creative director at GSD&M. He has spent the majority of his nearly 40 years in the business capturing the humanity of life on film for a multitude of clients. Much of it has focused on the business of the state of Texas, including Texas Tourism and most of the work for the legendary Don't Mess with Texas campaign. For the past eight months, Mike crisscrossed the state, searching for stories of faith of people from all walks of life and all religions. It was an amazing journey.

Randal Ford

RANDAL FORD

Randal Ford traversed Texas for over three months capturing the images within this book. With a passion for photography and a deep faith in God, Randal found this opportunity to photograph the people of Texas and its churches wholly inspiring. Originally from Dallas, he now lives in Austin. He received a business degree from Texas A&M University and has developed a career as a commercial and editorial photographer.

Mike Blair and Roy Spence

ACKNOWLEDGMENTS

We would like to thank the following individuals who have given their time and considerable talents to the creation of *The Amazing Faith of Texas*: David Crawford, Craig Denham, Libby DeLeon, Cyndi Hughes, Kelley Huston, Shannon McMillan, Diane Patrick, Kristi Robison, Haley Rushing, Robyn Schwartz, Anne Rix Sifuentez, Judy Trabulsi and Mara Truskoloski. Special thanks to CSI Printing in Austin, Texas, and especially to Chuck and Vance Sack. Their generous hearts and their company's uncompromising talent helped us produce the first edition of this beautiful book.

Oscar Vargas and Bob Decker

SPECIAL DEDICATION

We would like to dedicate this book to the faith of a family and the courage of a little boy. Oscar Vargas and his family are featured in the Bob Decker story about Paper Houses Across the Border. Oscar battled cancer for most of his young life. By the age of five, he had already survived six brain operations, chemotherapy and radiation. Yet his spirit was indomitable. Oscar taught us about faith and hope and the acceptance of God's will. He succumbed to the disease shortly after we went to press.

Abilene Columbus Fayetteville Gr
Eden Livingston Marathon Hico Te
Pyote Crystal City Coleman San
Ruidosa Sterling City Toyahvale
Palestine Sealy Buffalo Uvalde F
Del Rio Laredo Presidio Brenham S
New Salem Monahans Gruene Pan
Austin New Braunfels Snyder C
Alpine Sanderson Galveston Luli
Breckenridge Sweetwater Cuero Jun
Taylor Corpus Christi Jasper Sonor
Victoria Midland San Marcos Flat
Odessa Abilene Columbus Fayett
Columbus Fayetteville Graham
Livingston Marathon Hico Terli
Crystal City Coleman San Augus
Sterling City Toyahvale Lubbo